025
The A

Arnold Bennett

Coming Soon
How I Stole 5.6 Million from Walmart
The Gods Return Loki's Trial
Zombie Squirrels

Seattle, WA

The Author's Craft

Contents

Part I Seeing Life 5
    I 5
    II 9
    III 12
    IV 13
    V 16
    VI 17
    VII 20

Part II Writing Novels 23
    I 23
    II 26
    III 28
    IV 32
    V 37

Part III Writing Plays 41
    I 41
    II 43
    III 46
    IV 50
    V 53
    VI 55

Part IV The Artist and the Public 61
    I 61
    II 64
    III 68
    IV 72

The Author's Craft

Arnold Bennett

Part I Seeing Life

I

A young dog, inexperienced, sadly lacking in even primary education, ambles and frisks along the footpath of Fulham Road, near the mysterious gates of a Marist convent. He is a large puppy, on the way to be a dog of much dignity, but at present he has little to recommend him but that gawky elegance, and that bounding gratitude for the gift of life, which distinguish the normal puppy. He is an ignorant fool. He might have entered the convent of nuns and had a fine time, but instead he steps off the pavement into the road, the road being a vast and interesting continent imperfectly explored. His confidence in his nose, in his agility, and in the goodness of God is touching, absolutely painful to witness. He glances casually at a huge, towering vermilion construction that is whizzing towards him on four wheels, preceded by a glint of brass and a wisp of steam; and then with disdain he ignores it as less important than a mere speck of odorous matter in the mud. The next instant he is lying inert in the mud. His confidence in the goodness of God had been misplaced. Since the beginning of time God had ordained him a victim.

An impressive thing happens. The motor-bus reluctantly slackens and stops. Not the differential brake, nor the foot-brake, has arrested the motor-bus, but the invisible brake of public opinion, acting by administrative transmission. There is not a policeman in sight. Theoretically, the motor-'bus is free to whiz onward in its flight to the paradise of Shoreditch, but in practice it is paralysed by dread. A man in brass buttons and a stylish cap leaps down from it, and the blackened demon who sits on its neck also leaps down from it, and they move gingerly towards the puppy. A little while ago the motor-bus might have overturned a human cyclist or so, and proceeded nonchalant on its way. But now even a puppy requires a post-mortem: such is the force of public opinion aroused. Two policemen appear in the distance.

"A street accident" is now in being, and a crowd gathers with calm joy and stares, passive and determined. The puppy offers no sign whatever; just lies in the road. Then a boy, destined probably to a great future by reason of his singular faculty of initiative, goes to the puppy and carries him by the scruff of the neck, to the shelter of the gutter. Relinquished by the boy, the lithe puppy falls into an easy horizontal attitude, and seems bent upon repose. The boy lifts the puppy's head to examine it, and the head drops back wearily. The puppy is dead. No cry, no blood, no disfigurement! Even no perceptible jolt of the wheel as it climbed over the obstacle of the puppy's body! A wonderfully clean and perfect accident!

The increasing crowd stares with beatific placidity. People emerge impatiently from the bowels of the throbbing motor-bus and slip down from its back, and either join the crowd or vanish. The two policemen and the crew of the motor-bus have now met in parley. The conductor and the driver have an air at once nervous and resigned; their gestures are quick and vivacious. The policemen, on the other hand, indicate by their slow and huge movements that eternity is theirs. And they could not be more sure of the conductor and the driver if they had them manacled and leashed. The conductor and the driver admit the absolute dominion of the elephantine policemen; they admit that before the simple will of the policemen inconvenience, lost minutes, shortened leisure, docked wages, count as less than naught. And the policemen are carelessly sublime, well knowing that magistrates, jails, and the very Home Secretary on his throne—yes, and a whole system of conspiracy and perjury and brutality—are at their beck in case of need. And yet occasionally in the demeanour of the policemen towards the conductor and the driver there is a silent message that says: "After all, we, too, are working men like you, over-worked and under-paid and bursting with grievances in the service of the pitiless and dishonest public. We, too, have wives and children and privations and frightful apprehensions. We, too, have to struggle desperately. Only the awful magic of these garments and of the garter which we wear on our wrists sets an abyss between us and you." And the conductor writes and one of the policemen writes, and they keep on writing, while the traffic makes beautiful curves to avoid them.

The still increasing crowd continues to stare in the pure blankness of pleasure. A close-shaved, well-dressed, middle-aged man, with a copy of *The Sportsman* in his podgy hand, who has descended from the motor-bus, starts stamping his feet. "I was knocked down by a taxi last year," he says fiercely. "But nobody took no notice of *that*! Are they going to stop here all the blank morning for a blank tyke?" And for all his respectable appearance, his features become debased, and he emits a jet of disgusting profanity and brings most of the Trinity into the thunderous assertion that he has paid his fare. Then a man passes wheeling a muck-cart. And he stops and talks a long time with the other uniforms, because he, too, wears vestiges of a uniform. And the crowd never moves nor ceases to stare. Then the new arrival stoops and picks up the unclaimed, masterless puppy, and flings it, all soft and yielding, into the horrid mess of the cart, and passes on. And only that which is immortal and divine of the puppy remains behind, floating perhaps like an invisible vapour over the scene of the tragedy.

The Author's Craft

The crowd is tireless, all eyes. The four principals still converse and write. Nobody in the crowd comprehends what they are about. At length the driver separates himself, but is drawn back, and a new parley is commenced. But everything ends. The policemen turn on their immense heels. The driver and conductor race towards the motor-bus. The bell rings, the motor-bus, quite empty, disappears snorting round the corner into Walham Green. The crowd is now lessening. But it separates with reluctance, many of its members continuing to stare with intense absorption at the place where the puppy lay or the place where the policemen stood. An appreciable interval elapses before the "street accident" has entirely ceased to exist as a phenomenon.

The members of the crowd follow their noses, and during the course of the day remark to acquaintances:

"Saw a dog run over by a motor-bus in the Fulham Road this morning! Killed dead!"

And that is all they do remark. That is all they have witnessed. They will not, and could not, give intelligible and in teresting particulars of the affair (unless it were as to the breed of the dog or the number of the bus-service). They have watched a dog run over. They analyse neither their sensations nor the phenomenon. They have witnessed it whole, as a bad writer uses a *cliché* . They have observed—that is to say, they have really seen—nothing.

II

It will be well for us not to assume an attitude of condescension towards the crowd. Because in the matter of looking without seeing we are all about equal. We all go to and fro in a state of the observing faculties which somewhat resembles coma. We are all content to look and not see.

And if and when, having comprehended that the *rôle* of observer is not passive but active, we determine by an effort to rouse ourselves from the coma and really to see the spectacle of the world (a spectacle surpassing circuses and even street accidents in sustained dramatic interest), we shall discover, slowly in the course of time, that the act of seeing, which seems so easy, is not so easy as it seems. Let a man resolve: "I will keep my eyes open on the way to the office of a morning," and the probability if that for many mornings he will see naught that is not trivial, and that his system of perspective will be absurdly distorted. The unusual, the unaccustomed, will infallibly attract him, to the exclusion of what is fundamental and universal. Travel makes observers of us all, but the things which as travellers we observe generally show how unskilled we are in the new activity.

A man went to Paris for the first time, and observed right off that the carriages of suburban trains had seats on the roof like a tramcar. He was so thrilled by the remarkable discovery that he observed almost nothing else. This enormous fact occupied the whole foreground of his perspective. He returned home and announced that Paris was a place where people rode on the tops of trains. A Frenchwoman came to London for the first time—and no English person would ever guess the phenomenon which vanquished all others in her mind on the opening day. She saw a cat walking across a street. The vision

The Author's Craft

excited her. For in Paris cats do not roam in thoroughfares, because there are practically no houses with gardens or "areas"; the flat system is unfavourable to the enlargement of cats. I remember once, in the days when observation had first presented itself to me as a beautiful pastime, getting up very early and making the circuit of inner London before summer dawn in quest of interesting material. And the one note I gathered was that the ground in front of the all-night coffee-stalls was white with egg-shells! What I needed then was an operation for cataract. I also remember taking a man to the opera who had never seen an opera. The work was *Lohengrin* . When we came out he said: "That swan's neck was rather stiff." And it was all he did say. We went and had a drink. He was not mistaken. His observation was most just; but his perspective was that of those literary critics who give ten lines to point ing out three slips of syntax, and three lines to an ungrammatical admission that the novel under survey is not wholly tedious.

But a man may acquire the ability to observe even a large number of facts, and still remain in the infantile stage of observation. I have read, in some work of literary criticism, that Dickens could walk up one side of a long, busy street and down the other, and then tell you in their order the names on all the shop-signs; the fact was alleged as an illustration of his great powers of observation. Dickens was a great observer, but he would assuredly have been a still greater observer had he been a little less pre-occupied with trivial and unco-ordinated details. Good observation consists not in multiplicity of detail, but in co-ordination of detail according to a true perspective of relative importance, so that a finally just general impression may be reached in the shortest possible time. The skilled observer is he who does not have to change his mind. One has only to compare one's present adjusted impression of an intimate friend with one's first impression of him to perceive the astounding inadequacy of one's powers of observation. The man as one has learnt to see him is simply not the same man who walked into one's drawing-room on the day of introduction.

There are, by the way, three sorts of created beings who are sentimentally supposed to be able to judge individuals at the first glance: women, children, and dogs. By virtue of a mystic gift with which rumour credits them, they are never mistaken. It is merely not true. Women are constantly quite wrong in the estimates based on their "feminine instinct"; they sometimes even admit it; and the matrimonial courts prove it *passim* . Children are more often wrong than women. And as for dogs, it is notorious that they are for ever being taken in by plausible scoundrels; the perspective of dogs is grotesque. Not seldom have I grimly watched the gradual disillusion of deceived dogs. Nevertheless, the sentimental legend of the infallibility of women, children, and dogs, will persist in Anglo-Saxon countries.

The Author's Craft
III

One is curious about one's fellow-creatures: therefore one watches them. And generally the more intelligent one is, the more curious one is, and the more one observes. The mere satisfaction of this curiosity is in itself a worthy end, and would alone justify the business of systematised observation. But the aim of observation may, and should, be expressed in terms more grandiose. Human curiosity counts among the highest social virtues (as indifference counts among the basest defects), because it leads to the disclosure of the causes of character and temperament and thereby to a better understanding of the springs of human conduct. Observation is not practised directly with this high end in view (save by prigs and other futile souls); nevertheless it is a moral act and must inevitably promote kindliness—whether we like it or not. It also sharpens the sense of beauty. An ugly deed—such as a deed of cruelty—takes on artistic beauty when its origin and hence its fitness in the general scheme begin to be comprehended. In the perspective of history we can derive an æsthetic pleasure from the tranquil scrutiny of all kinds of conduct—as well, for example, of a Renaissance Pope as of a Savonarola. Observation endows our day and our street with the romantic charm of history, and stimulates charity—not the charity which signs cheques, but the more precious charity which puts itself to the trouble of understanding. The one condition is that the observer must never lose sight of the fact that what he is trying to see is life, is the woman next door, is the man in the train—and not a concourse of abstractions. To appreciate all this is the first inspiring preliminary to sound observation.

IV

The second preliminary is to realise that all physical phenomena are interrelated, that there is nothing which does not bear on everything else. The whole spectacular and sensual show—what the eye sees, the ear hears, the nose scents, the tongue tastes and the skin touches—is a cause or an effect of human conduct. Naught can be ruled out as negligible, as not forming part of the equation. Hence he who would beyond all others see life for himself—I naturally mean the novelist and playwright—ought to embrace all phenomena in his curiosity. Being finite, he cannot. Of course he cannot! But he can, by obtaining a broad notion of the whole, determine with some accuracy the position and relative importance of the particular series of phenomena to which his instinct draws him. If he does not thus envisage the immense background of his special interests, he will lose the most precious feeling for interplay and proportion without which all specialism becomes distorted and positively darkened.

Now, the main factor in life on this planet is the planet itself. Any logically conceived survey of existence must begin with geographical and climatic phenomena. This is surely obvious. If you say that you are not interested in meteorology or the configurations of the earth, I say that you deceive yourself. You are. For an east wind may upset your liver and cause you to insult your wife. Beyond question the most important fact about, for example, Great Britain is that it is an island. We sail amid the Hebrides, and then talk of the fine qualities and the distressing limitations of those islanders; it ought to occur to us English that we are talking of ourselves in little. In moments of journalistic vainglory we are apt to refer to the "sturdy island race," meaning us. But that we are insular in the full significance of the horrid word is certain. Why not? A genuine observation of the supreme phenomenon that Great Britain is surrounded by water—an effort to keep it always at the back of the consciousness—will help to explain all the minor phenomena of British existence. Geographical knowledge is the mother of discernment, for the varying physical characteristics of the earth are the sole direct terrestrial influence determining the evolution of original vital energy.

    All other influences are secondary, and have been effects of character and temperament before becoming causes. Perhaps the greatest of them are roads and architecture. Nothing could be more English than English roads, or more French than French roads. Enter England from France, let us say through the gate of Folkestone, and the architectural illustration which greets you (if you can look and see) is absolutely dramatic in its spectacular force. You say that there is no architecture in Folkestone. But Folkestone, like other towns, is just as full of architecture as a wood is full of trees. As the train winds on its causeway over the sloping town you perceive below you thousands of squat little homes, neat, tended, respectable, comfortable, prim, at once unostentatious and conceited. Each a separate, clearly-defined entity! Each saying to the others: "Don't look over my wall, and I won't look over yours!" Each with a ferocious jealousy bent on guarding its own individuality! Each a stronghold—an island! And all careless of the general effect, but making a very impressive general effect. The English race is below you. Your own son is below you insisting on the inviolability of his own den of a bedroom! ... And contrast all that with the immense communistic and splendid façades of a French town, and work out the implications. If you really intend to see life you cannot afford to be blind to such thrilling phenomena.

Arnold Bennett

Yet an inexperienced, unguided curiosity would be capable of walking through a French street and through an English street, and noting chiefly that whereas English lamp-posts spring from the kerb, French lamp-posts cling to the side of the house! Not that that detail is not worth noting. It is—in its place. French lamp-posts are part of what we call the "interesting character" of a French street. We say of a French street that it is "full of character." As if an English street was not! Such is blindness—to be cured by travel and the exercise of the logical faculty, most properly termed common sense. If one is struck by the magnificence of the great towns of the Continent, one should ratiocinate, and conclude that a major characteristic of the great towns of England is their shabby and higgledy-piggledy slovenliness. It is so. But there are people who have lived fifty years in Manchester, Leeds, Hull and Hanley without noticing it. The English idiosyncrasy is in that awful external slovenliness too, causing it, and being caused by it. Every street is a mirror, an illustration, an exposition, an explanation, of the human beings who live in it. Nothing in it is to be neglected. Everything in it is valuable, if the perspective is maintained. Nevertheless, in the narrow individualistic novels of English literature—and in some of the best— you will find a domestic organism described as though it existed in a vacuum, or in the Sahara, or between Heaven and earth; as though it reacted on nothing and was reacted on by nothing; and as though it could be adequately rendered without reference to anything exterior to itself. How can such novels satisfy a reader who has acquired or wants to acquire the faculty of seeing life?

The Author's Craft
V

The net result of the interplay of instincts and influences which determine the existence of a community is shown in the general expression on the faces of the people. This is an index which cannot lie and cannot be gainsaid. It is fairly easy, and extremely interesting, to decipher. It is so open, shameless, and universal, that not to look at it is impossible. Yet the majority of persons fail to see it. We hear of inquirers standing on London Bridge and counting the number of motor-buses, foot-passengers, lorries, and white horses that pass over the bridge in an hour. But we never hear of anybody counting the number of faces happy or unhappy, honest or rascally, shrewd or ingenuous, kind or cruel, that pass over the bridge. Perhaps the public may be surprised to hear that the general ex pression on the faces of Londoners of all ranks varies from the sad to the morose; and that their general mien is one of haste and gloomy preoccupation. Such a staring fact is paramount in sociological evidence. And the observer of it would be justified in summoning Heaven, the legislature, the county council, the churches, and the ruling classes, and saying to them: "Glance at these faces, and don't boast too much about what you have accomplished. The climate and the industrial system have so far triumphed over you all."

Arnold Bennett
VI

When we come to the observing of the individual—to which all human observing does finally come if there is any right reason in it—the aforesaid general considerations ought to be ever present in the hinterland of the consciousness, aiding and influencing, perhaps vaguely, perhaps almost imperceptibly, the formation of judgments. If they do nothing else, they will at any rate accustom the observer to the highly important idea of the correlation of all phenomena. Especially in England a haphazard particularity is the chief vitiating element in the operations of the mind.

In estimating the individual we are apt not only to forget his environment, but—really strange!—to ignore much of the evidence visible in the individual himself. The inexperienced and ardent observer, will, for example, be astonishingly blind to everything in an individual except his face. Telling himself that the face must be the reflection of the soul, and that every thought and emotion leaves inevitably its mark there, he will concentrate on the face, singling it out as a phenomenon apart and self-complete. Were he a god and infallible, he could no doubt learn the whole truth from the face. But he is bound to fall into errors, and by limiting the field of vision he minimises the opportunity for correction. The face is, after all, quite a small part of the individual's physical organism. An Englishman will look at a woman's face and say she is a beautiful woman or a plain woman. But a woman may have a plain face, and yet by her form be entitled to be called beautiful, and (perhaps) *vice versâ*. It is true that the face is the reflexion of the soul. It is equally true that the carriage and gestures are the reflection of the soul. Had one eyes, the tying of a bootlace is the reflection of the soul. One piece of evidence can be used to correct every other piece of evidence. A refined face may be refuted by clumsy finger-ends; the eyes may contradict the voice; the gait may nullify the smile. None of the phenomena which every individual carelessly and brazenly displays in every motor-bus terrorising the streets of London is meaningless or negligible.

Again, in observing we are generally guilty of that particularity which results from sluggishness of the imagination. We may see the phenomenon at the moment of looking at it, but we particularise in that moment, making no effort to conceive what the phenomenon is likely to be at other moments.

For example, a male human creature wakes up in the morning and rises with reluctance. Being a big man, and existing with his wife and children in a very confined space, he has to adapt himself to his environment as he goes through the various functions incident to preparing for his day's work. He is just like you or me. He wants his breakfast, he very much wants to know where his boots are, and he has the usually sinister preoccupations about health and finance. Whatever the force of his egoism, he must more or less harmonise his individuality with those of his wife and children. Having laid down the law, or accepted it, he sets forth to his daily duties, just a fraction of a minute late. He arrives at his office, resumes life with his colleagues sympathetic and antipathetic, and then leaves the office for an expedition extending over several hours. In the course of his expedition he encounters the corpse of a young dog run down by a motor-bus. Now you also have encountered that corpse and are gazing at it; and what do you say to yourself when he comes along? You say: "Oh! Here's a policeman." For he happens to be a policeman. You stare at him, and you never see anything but a policeman—an indivisible phenomenon of blue cloth, steel buttons, flesh resembling a face, and a helmet; " a stalwart guardian of the law"; to you little more human than an algebraic symbol: in a word—a policeman.

Only, that word actually conveys almost nothing to you of the reality which it stands for. You are satisfied with it as you are satisfied with the description of a disease. A friend tells you his eyesight is failing. You sympathise. "What is it?" you ask. "Glaucoma." "Ah! Glaucoma!" You don't know what glaucoma is. You are no wiser than you were before. But you are content. A name has contented you. Similarly the name of policeman contents you, seems to absolve you from further curiosity as to the phenomenon. You have looked at tens of thousands of policemen, and perhaps never seen the hundredth part of the reality of a single one. Your imagination has not truly worked on the phenomenon.

There may be some excuse for not seeing the reality of a policeman, because a uniform is always a thick veil. But you — I mean you, I, any of us—are oddly dim-sighted also in regard to the civil population. For instance, we get into the empty motor-bus as it leaves the scene of the street accident, and examine the men and women who gradually fill it. Probably we vaunt ourselves as being interested in the spectacle of life. All the persons in the motor-bus have come out of a past and are moving towards a future. But how often does our imagination put itself to the trouble of realising this? We may observe with some care, yet owing to a fundamental defect of attitude we are observing not the human individuals, but a peculiar race of beings who pass their whole lives in motor-buses, who exist only in motor-buses and only in the present! No human phenomenon is adequately seen until the imagination has placed it back into its past and forward into its future. And this is the final process of observation of the individual.

VII

Seeing life, as I have tried to show, does not begin with seeing the individual. Neither does it end with seeing the individual. Particular and unsystematised observation cannot go on for ever, aimless, formless. Just as individuals are singled out from systems, in the earlier process of observation, so in the later processes individuals will be formed into new groups, which formation will depend upon the personal bent of the observer. The predominant interests of the observer will ultimately direct his observing activities to their own advantage. If he is excited by the phenomena of organisation—as I happen to be—he will see individuals in new groups that are the result of organisation, and will insist on the variations from type due to that grouping. If he is convinced—as numbers of people appear to be—that society is just now in an extremely critical pass, and that if something mysterious is not forthwith done the structure of it will crumble to atoms—he will see mankind grouped under the different reforms which, according to him, the human dilemma demands. And so on! These tendencies, while they should not be resisted too much, since they give character to observation and redeem it from the frigidity of mechanics, should be resisted to a certain extent. For, whatever they may be, they favour the growth of sentimentality, the protean and indescribably subtle enemy of common sense.

Arnold Bennett

The Author's Craft

Arnold Bennett

Part II Writing Novels

I

The novelist is he who, having seen life, and being so excited by it that he absolutely must transmit the vision to others, chooses narrative fiction as the liveliest vehicle for the relief of his feelings. He is like other artists—he cannot remain silent; he cannot keep himself to himself, he is bursting with the news; he is bound to tell—the affair is too thrilling! Only he differs from most artists in this—that what most chiefly strikes him is the indefinable humanness of human nature, the large general manner of existing. Of course, he is the result of evolution from the primitive. And you can see primitive novelists to this day transmitting to acquaintances their fragmentary and crude visions of life in the café or the club, or on the kerbstone. They belong to the lowest circle of artists; but they are artists; and the form that they adopt is the very basis of the novel. By innumerable entertaining steps from them you may ascend to the major artist whose vision of life, inclusive, intricate and intense, requires for its due transmission the great traditional form of the novel as perfected by the masters of a long age which has temporarily set the novel higher than any other art-form.

I would not argue that the novel should be counted supreme among the great traditional forms of art. Even if there is a greatest form, I do not much care which it is. I have in turn been convinced that Chartres Cathedral, certain Greek sculpture, Mozart's *Don Juan* , and the juggling of Paul Cinquevalli, was the finest thing in the world—not to mention the achievements of Shakspere or

Nijinsky. But there is something to be said for the real pre-eminence of prose fiction as a literary form. (Even the modern epic has learnt almost all it knows from prose-fiction.) The novel has, and always will have, the advantage of its comprehensive bigness. St Peter's at Rome is a trifle compared with Tolstoi's *War and Peace* ; and it is as certain as anything can be that, during the present geological epoch at any rate, no epic half as long as *War and Peace* will ever be read, even if written.

    Notoriously the novelist (including the playwright, who is a sub-novelist) has been taking the bread out of the mouths of other artists. In the matter of poaching, the painter has done a lot, and the composer has done more, but what the painter and the composer have done is as naught compared to the grasping deeds of the novelist. And whereas the painter and the composer have got into difficulties with their audacious schemes, the novelist has poached, colonised, and annexed with a success that is not denied. There is scarcely any aspect of the interestingness of life which is not now rendered in prose fiction—from landscape-painting to sociology—and none which might not be. Unnecessary to go back to the ante-Scott age in order to perceive how the novel has aggrandised itself! It has conquered enormous territories even since *Germinal* . Within the last fifteen years it has gained. Were it to adopt the hue of the British Empire, the entire map of the universe would soon be coloured red. Wherever it ought to stand in the hierarchy of forms, it has, actually, no rival at the present day as a means for transmitting the impassioned vision of life. It is, and will be for some time to come, the form to which the artist with the most inclusive vision instinctively turns, because it is the most inclusive form, and the most adaptable. Indeed, before we are much older, if its present rate of progress continues, it will have reoccupied the dazzling position to which the mighty Balzac lifted it, and in which he left it in 1850. So much, by the way, for the rank of the novel.

The Author's Craft
II

In considering the equipment of the novelist there are two attributes which may always be taken for granted. The first is the sense of beauty—indispensable to the creative artist. Every creative artist has it, in his degree. He is an artist because he has it. An artist works under the stress of instinct. No man's instinct can draw him towards material which repels him—the fact is obvious. Obviously, whatever kind of life the novelist writes about, he has been charmed and seduced by it, he is under its spell—that is, he has seen beauty in it. He could have no other reason for writing about it. He may see a strange sort of beauty; he may—indeed he does—see a sort of beauty that nobody has quite seen before; he may see a sort of beauty that none save a few odd spirits ever will or can be made to see. But he does see beauty. To say, after reading a novel which has held you, that the author has no sense of beauty, is inept. (The mere fact that you turned over his pages with interest is an answer to the criticism—a criticism, indeed, which is not more sagacious than that of the reviewer who remarks: "Mr Blank has produced a thrilling novel, but unfortunately he cannot write." Mr Blank has written; and he could, anyhow, write enough to thrill the reviewer.) All that a wise person will assert is that an artist's sense of beauty is different for the time being from his own.

The reproach of the lack of a sense of beauty has been brought against nearly all original novelists; it is seldom brought against a mediocre novelist. Even in the extreme cases it is untrue; perhaps it is most untrue in the extreme cases. I do not mean such a case as that of Zola, who never went to extremes. I mean, for example, Gissing, a real extremist, who, it is now admitted, saw a clear and undiscovered beauty in forms of existence which hitherto no artist had deigned seriously to examine. And I mean

Huysmans, a case even more extreme. Possibly no works have been more abused for ugliness than Huysman's novel *En Ménage* and his book of descriptive essays *De Tout*. Both reproduce with exasperation what is generally regarded as the sordid ugliness of commonplace daily life. Yet both exercise a unique charm (and will surely be read when *La Cathédrale* is forgotten). And it is inconceivable that Huysmans—whatever he may have said—was not ravished by the secret beauty of his subjects and did not exult in it.

The other attribute which may be taken for granted in the novelist, as in every artist, is passionate intensity of vision. Unless the vision is passionately intense the artist will not be moved to transmit it. He will not be inconvenienced by it; and the motive to pass it on will thus not exist. Every fine emotion produced in the reader has been, and must have been, previously felt by the writer, but in a far greater degree. It is not altogether uncommon to hear a reader whose heart has been desolated by the poignancy of a narrative complain that the writer is unemotional. Such people have no notion at all of the processes of artistic creation.

The Author's Craft
III

A sense of beauty and a passionate intensity of vision being taken for granted, the one other important attribute in the equipment of the novelist—the attribute which indeed by itself practically suffices, and whose absence renders futile all the rest—is fineness of mind. A great novelist must have great qualities of mind. His mind must be sympathetic, quickly responsive, courageous, honest, humorous, tender, just, merciful. He must be able to conceive the ideal without losing sight of the fact that it is a human world we live in. Above all, his mind must be permeated and controlled by common sense. His mind, in a word, must have the quality of being noble. Unless his mind is all this, he will never, at the ultimate bar, be reckoned supreme. That which counts, on every page, and all the time, is the very texture of his mind—the glass through which he sees things. Every other attribute is secondary, and is dispensable. Fielding lives unequalled among English novelists because the broad nobility of his mind is unequalled. He is read with unreserved enthusiasm because the reader feels himself at each paragraph to be in close contact with a glorious personality. And no advance in technique among later novelists can possibly imperil his position. He will take second place when a more noble mind, a more superb common sense, happens to wield the narrative pen, and not before. What undermines the renown of Dickens is the growing conviction that the texture of his mind was common, that he fell short in courageous facing of the truth, and in certain delicacies of perception. As much may be said of Thackeray, whose mind was somewhat incomplete for so grandiose a figure, and not free from defects which are inimical to immortality.

It is a hard saying for me, and full of danger in any country whose artists have shown contempt for form, yet I am obliged to say that, as the years pass, I attach less and less importance to good technique in fiction. I love it, and I have fought for a better recognition of its importance in England, but I now have to admit that the modern history of fiction will not support me. With the single exception of Turgenev, the great novelists of the world, according to my own standards, have either ignored technique or have failed to understand it. What an error to suppose that the finest foreign novels show a better sense of form than the finest English novels! Balzac was a prodigious blunderer. He could not even manage a sentence, not to speak of the general form of a book. And as for a greater than Balzac—Stendhal—his scorn of technique was notorious. Stendhal was capable of writing, in a masterpiece: "By the way I ought to have told you earlier that the Duchess—!" And as for a greater than either Balzac or Stendhal—Dostoievsky—what a hasty, amorphous lump of gold is the sublime, the unapproachable *Brothers Karamazov* ! Any tutor in a college for teaching the whole art of fiction by post in twelve lessons could show where Dostoievsky was clumsy and careless. What would have been Flaubert's detailed criticism of that book? And what would it matter? And, to take a minor example, witness the comically amateurish technique of the late "Mark Rutherford"—nevertheless a novelist whom one can deeply admire.

And when we come to consider the great technicians, Guy de Maupassant and Flaubert, can we say that their technique will save them, or atone in the slightest degree for the defects of their minds? Exceptional artists both, they are both now inevitably falling in esteem to the level of the second-rate. Human nature being what it is, and de Maupassant being tinged with eroticism, his work is sure to be read with interest by mankind; but he is already classed. Nobody, now, despite all his brilliant excellences, would dream of putting de Maupassant with the first magnitudes. And the declension of Flaubert is one of the outstanding phenomena of modern French criticism. It is being discovered that Flaubert's mind was not quite noble enough—that, indeed, it was a cruel mind, and a little anæmic. *Bouvard et Pécuchet* was the crowning proof that Flaubert had lost sight of the humanness of the world, and suffered from the delusion that he had been born on the wrong planet. The glitter of his technique is dulled now, and fools even count it against him. In regard to one section of human activity only did his mind seem noble—namely, literary technique. His correspondence, written, of course, currently, was largely occupied with the question of literary technique, and his correspondence stands forth to-day as his best work—a marvellous fount of inspiration to his fellow artists. So I return to the point that the novelist's one important attribute (beyond the two postulated) is fundamental quality of mind. It and nothing else makes both the friends and the enemies which he has; while the influence of technique is slight and transitory. And I repeat that it is a hard saying.

    I begin to think that great writers of fiction are by the mysterious nature of their art ordained to be "amateurs." There may be something of the amateur in all great artists. I do not know why it should be so, unless because, in the exuberance of their sense of power, they are impatient of the exactitudes of systematic study and the mere bother of repeated attempts to arrive at a minor perfection. Assuredly no great artist was ever a profound scholar. The great artist has other ends to achieve. And every artist, major and minor, is aware in his conscience that art is full of artifice, and that the desire to proceed rapidly with the affair of creation, and an excus able dislike of re-creating anything twice, thrice, or ten times over—unnatural task!—are responsible for much of that artifice. We can all point in excuse to Shakspere, who was a very rough-and-ready person, and whose methods would shock Flaubert. Indeed, the amateurishness of Shakspere has been mightily exposed of late years. But nobody seems to care. If Flaubert had been a greater artist he might have been more of an amateur.

The Author's Craft
IV

Of this poor neglected matter of technique the more important branch is design—or construction. It is the branch of the art—of all arts—which comes next after "inspiration"—a capacious word meant to include everything that the artist must be born with and cannot acquire. The less important branch of technique—far less important—may be described as an ornamentation.

There are very few rules of design in the novel; but the few are capital. Nevertheless, great novelists have often flouted or ignored them—to the detriment of their work. In my opinion the first rule is that the interest must be centralised; it must not be diffused equally over various parts of the canvas. To compare one art with another may be perilous, but really the convenience of describing a novel as a canvas is extreme. In a well-designed picture the eye is drawn chiefly to one particular spot. If the eye is drawn with equal force to several different spots, then we reproach the painter for having "scattered" the interest of the picture. Similarly with the novel. A novel must have one, two, or three figures that easily overtop the rest. These figures must be in the foreground, and the rest in the middle-distance or in the back-ground.

Moreover, these figures—whether they are saints or sinners—must somehow be presented more sympathetically than the others. If this cannot be done, then the inspiration is at fault. The single motive that should govern the choice of a principal figure is the motive of love for that figure. What else could the motive be? The race of heroes is essential to art. But what makes a hero is less the deeds of the figure chosen than the understanding sympathy of the artist with the figure. To say that the hero has disappeared from modern fiction is absurd. All that has happened is that the characteristics of the hero have changed, naturally, with the times. When Thackeray wrote "a novel without a hero," he wrote a novel with a first-class hero, and nobody knew this better than Thackeray. What he meant was that he was sick of the conventional bundle of characteristics styled a hero in his day, and that he had changed the type. Since then we have grown sick of Dobbins, and the type has been changed again more than once. The fateful hour will arrive when we shall be sick of Ponderevos.

The temptation of the great novelist, overflowing with creative force, is to scatter the interest. In both his major works Tolstoi found the temptation too strong for him. *Anna Karenina* is not one novel, but two, and suffers accordingly. As for *War and Peace* , the reader wanders about in it as in a forest, for days, lost, deprived of a sense of direction, and with no vestige of a sign-post; at intervals encountering mysterious faces whose identity he in vain tries to recall. On a much smaller scale Meredith committed the same error. Who could assert positively which of the sisters Fleming is the heroine of *Rhoda Fleming* ? For nearly two hundred pages at a stretch Rhoda scarcely appears. And more than once the author seems quite to forget that the little knave Algernon is not, after all, the hero of the story.

The second rule of design—perhaps in the main merely a different view of the first—is that the interest must be maintained. It may increase, but it must never diminish. Here is that special aspect of design which we call construction, or plot. By interest I mean the interest of the story itself, and not the interest of the continual play of the author's mind on his material. In proportion as the interest of the story is maintained, the plot is a good one. In so far as it lapses, the plot is a bad one. There is no other criterion of good con struction. Readers of a certain class are apt to call good the plot of that story in which

The Author's Craft

"you can't tell what is going to happen next." But in some of the most tedious novels ever written you can't tell what is going to happen next—and you don't care a fig what is going to happen next. It would be nearer the mark to say that the plot is good when "you want to make sure what will happen next"! Good plots set you anxiously guessing what will happen next.

When the reader is misled—not intentionally in order to get an effect, but clumsily through amateurishness—then the construction is bad. This calamity does not often occur in fine novels, but in really good work another calamity does occur with far too much frequency—namely, the tantalising of the reader at a critical point by a purposeless, wanton, or negligent shifting of the interest from the major to the minor theme. A sad example of this infantile trick is to be found in the thirty-first chapter of *Rhoda Fleming* , wherein, well knowing that the reader is tingling for the interview between Roberts and Rhoda, the author, unable to control his own capricious and monstrous fancy for Algernon, devotes some sixteen pages to the young knave's vagaries with an illicit thousand pounds. That the sixteen pages are excessively brilliant does not a bit excuse the wilful unshapeliness of the book's design.

The Edwardian and Georgian out-and-out defenders of Victorian fiction are wont to argue that though the event-plot in sundry great novels may be loose and casual (that is to say, simply careless), the "idea-plot" is usually close-knit, coherent, and logical. I have never yet been able to comprehend how an idea-plot can exist independently of an event-plot (any more than how spirit can be conceived apart from matter); but assuming that an idea-plot can exist independently, and that the mysterious thing is superior in form to its coarse fellow, the event-plot (which I positively do not believe),—even then I still hold that sloppiness in the fabrication of the event-plot amounts to a grave iniquity. In this connection I have in mind, among English novels, chiefly the work of "Mark Rutherford," George Eliot, the Brontës, and Anthony Trollope.

The one other important rule in construction is that the plot should be kept throughout within the same convention. All plots—even those of our most sacred naturalistic contemporaries—are and must be a conventionalisation of life. We imagine we have arrived at a convention which is nearer to the truth of life than that of our forerunners. Perhaps we have—but so little nearer that the difference is scarcely appreciable! An aviator at midday may be nearer the sun than the motorist, but regarded as a portion of the entire journey to the sun, the aviator's progress upward can safely be ignored. No novelist has yet, or ever will, come within a hundred million miles of life itself. It is impossible for us to see how far we still are from life. The defects of a new convention disclose themselves late in its career. The notion that "naturalists" have at last lighted on a final formula which ensures truth to life is ridiculous. "Naturalist" is merely an epithet expressing self-satisfaction.

Similarly, the habit of deriding as "conventional" plots constructed in an earlier convention, is ridiculous. Under this head Dickens in particular has been assaulted; I have assaulted him myself. But within their convention, the plots of Dickens are excellent, and show little trace of amateurishness, and every sign of skilled accomplishment. And Dickens did not blunder out of one convention into another, as certain of ourselves undeniably do. Thomas Hardy, too, has been arraigned for the conventionalism of his plots. And yet Hardy happens to be one of the rare novelists who have evolved a new convention to suit their idiosyncrasy. Hardy's idiosyncrasy is a deep conviction of the whimsicality of the divine power, and again and again he has expressed this with a virtuosity of skill which ought to have put humility into the hearts of naturalists, but which has not done so. The plot of *The Woodlanders* is one of the most exquisite examples of subtle symbolic illustration of an idea that a writer of fiction ever achieved; it makes the symbolism of Ibsen seem crude. You may say that *The Woodlanders* could not have occurred in real life. No novel could have occurred in real life. The balance of probabilities is incalculably against any novel whatsoever; and rightly so. A convention is essential, and the duty of a novelist is to be true within his chosen convention, and not further. Most novelists still fail in this duty. Is there any reason, indeed, why we should be so vastly cleverer than our fathers? I do not think we are.

Arnold Bennett

V

Leaving the seductive minor question of ornamentation, I come lastly to the question of getting the semblance of life on to the page before the eyes of the reader—the daily and hourly texture of existence. The novelist has selected his subject; he has drenched himself in his subject. He has laid down the main features of the design. The living embryo is there, and waits to be developed into full organic structure. Whence and how does the novelist obtain the vital tissue which must be his material? The answer is that he digs it out of himself. First-class fiction is, and must be, in the final resort autobiographical. What else should it be? The novelist may take notes of phenomena likely to be of use to him. And he may acquire the skill to invent very apposite illustrative inci dent. But he cannot invent psychology. Upon occasion some human being may entrust him with confidences extremely precious for his craft. But such windfalls are so rare as to be negligible. From outward symptoms he can guess something of the psychology of others. He can use a real person as the unrecognisable but helpful basis for each of his characters.... And all that is nothing. And all special research is nothing. When the real intimate work of creation has to be done—and it has to be done on every page—the novelist can only look within for effective aid. Almost solely by arranging and modifying what he has felt and seen, and scarcely at all by inventing, can he accomplish his end. An inquiry into the career of any first-class novelist invariably reveals that his novels are full of autobiography. But, as a fact, every good novel contains far more autobiography than any inquiry could reveal. Episodes, moods, characters of autobiography can be detected and traced to their origin by critical acumen, but the intimate autobiography that runs through each page, vitalising it, may not be detected. In dealing with each character in each episode the novelist

The Author's Craft

must for a thousand convincing details interrogate that part of his own individuality which corresponds to the particular character. The foundation of his equipment is universal sympathy. And the result of this (or the cause—I don't know which) is that in his own individuality there is something of everybody. If he is a born novelist he is safe in asking himself, when in doubt as to the behaviour of a given personage at a given point: "Now, what should *I* have done?" And incorporating the answer! And this in practice is what he does. Good fiction is autobiography dressed in the colours of all mankind.

The necessarily autobiographical nature of fiction accounts for the creative repetition to which all novelists—including the most powerful—are reduced. They monotonously yield again and again to the strongest predilections of their own individuality. Again and again they think they are creating, by observation, a quite new character—and lo! when finished it is an old one—autobiographical psychology has triumphed! A novelist may achieve a reputation with only a single type, created and re-created in varying forms. And the very greatest do not contrive to create more than half a score genuine separate types. In Cerfberr and Christophe's biographical dictionary of the characters of Balzac, a tall volume of six hundred pages, there are some two thousand entries of different individuals, but probably fewer than a dozen genuine distinctive types. No creative artist ever repeated himself more brazenly or more successfully than Balzac. His miser, his vicious delightful actress, his vicious delightful duchess, his young man-about-town, his virtuous young man, his heroic weeping virgin, his angelic wife and mother, his poor relation, and his faithful stupid servant—each is continually popping up with a new name in the Human Comedy. A similar phenomenon, as Frank Harris has proved, is to be observed in Shakspere. Hamlet of Denmark was only the last and greatest of a series of Shaksperean Hamlets.

Arnold Bennett

It may be asked, finally: What of the actual process of handling the raw material dug out of existence and of the artist's self—the process of transmuting life into art? There is no process. That is to say, there is no conscious process. The convention chosen by an artist is his illusion of the truth. Consciously, the artist only omits, selects, arranges. But let him beware of being false to his illusion, for then the process becomes conscious, and bad. This is sentimentality, which is the seed of death in his work. Every artist is tempted to sentimentalise, or to be cynical—practically the same thing. And when he falls to the temptation, the reader whispers in his heart, be it only for one instant: "That is not true to life." And in turn the reader's illusion of reality is impaired. Readers are divided into two classes—the enemies and the friends of the artist. The former, a legion, admire for a fortnight or a year. They hate an uncompromising struggle for the truth. They positively like the artist to fall to temptation. If he falls, they exclaim, "How sweet!" The latter are capable of savouring the fine unpleasantness of the struggle for truth. And when they whisper in their hearts: "That is not true to life," they are ashamed for the artist. They are few, very few; but a vigorous clan. It is they who confer immortality.

The Author's Craft

Arnold Bennett

Part III Writing Plays

I

There is an idea abroad, assiduously fostered as a rule by critics who happen to have written neither novels nor plays, that it is more difficult to write a play than a novel. I do not think so. I have written or collaborated in about twenty novels and about twenty plays, and I am convinced that it is easier to write a play than a novel. Personally, I would sooner *write* two plays than one novel; less expenditure of nervous force and mere brains would be required for two plays than for one novel. (I emphasise the word "write," because if the whole weariness between the first conception and the first performance of a play is compared with the whole weariness between the first conception and the first publication of a novel, then the play has it. I would sooner get seventy-and-seven novels produced than one play. But my immediate object is to compare only writing with writing.) It seems to me that the sole persons entitled to judge of the comparative difficulty of writing plays and writing novels are those authors who have succeeded or failed equally well in both departments. And in this limited band I imagine that the differences of opinion on the point could not be marked. I would like to note in passing, for the support of my proposition, that whereas established novelists not infrequently venture into the theatre with audacity, established dramatists are very cautious indeed about quitting the theatre. An established dramatist usually takes good care to write plays and naught else; he will not affront the risks of coming out into the open; and therein his instinct is quite properly that of self-preservation. Of many established dramatists all over the world it may be affirmed that if they were so indiscreet as to publish a novel, the result would be a great shattering and a great awakening.

II

An enormous amount of vague reverential nonsense is talked about the technique of the stage, the assumption being that in difficulty it far surpasses any other literary technique, and that until it is acquired a respectable play cannot be written. One hears also that it can only be acquired behind the scenes. A famous actor-manager once kindly gave me the benefit of his experience, and what he said was that a dramatist who wished to learn his business must live behind the scenes—and study the works of Dion Boucicault! The truth is that no technique is so crude and so simple as the technique of the stage, and that the proper place to learn it is not behind the scenes but in the pit. Managers, being the most conservative people on earth, except compositors, will honestly try to convince the naïve dramatist that effects can only be obtained in the precise way in which effects have always been obtained, and that this and that rule must not be broken on pain of outraging the public.

And indeed it is natural that managers should talk thus, seeing the low state of the drama, because in any art rules and reaction always flourish when creative energy is sick. The mandarins have ever said and will ever say that a technique which does not correspond with their own is no technique, but simple clumsiness. There are some seven situations in the customary drama, and a play which does not contain at least one of those situations in each act will be condemned as "undramatic," or "thin," or as being "all talk." It may contain half a hundred other situations, but for the mandarin a situation which is not one of the seven is not a situation. Similarly there are some dozen character types in the customary drama, and all original that is, truthful—characterisation will be dismissed as a total absence of characterisation because it does not reproduce any of these dozen types. Thus every truly

The Author's Craft

original play is bound to be indicted for bad technique. The author is bound to be told that what he has written may be marvellously clever, but that it is not a play. I remember the day—and it is not long ago—when even so experienced and sincere a critic as William Archer used to argue that if the "intellectual" drama did not succeed with the general public, it was because its technique was not up to the level of the technique of the commercial drama! Perhaps he has changed his opinion since then. Heaven knows that the so-called "intellectual" drama is amateurish enough, but nearly all literary art is amateurish, and assuredly no intellectual drama could hope to compete in clumsiness with some of the most successful commercial plays of modern times. I tremble to think what the mandarins and William Archer would say to the technique of *Hamlet* , could it by some miracle be brought forward as a new piece by a Mr Shakspere. They would probably recommend Mr Shakspere to consider the ways of Sardou, Henri Bernstein, and Sir Herbert Tree, and be wise. Most positively they would assert that *Hamlet* was not a play. And their pupils of the daily press would point out—what surely Mr Shakspere ought to have perceived for himself—that the second, third, or fourth act might be cut wholesale without the slightest loss to the piece.

In the sense in which mandarins understand the word technique, there is no technique special to the stage except that which concerns the moving of solid human bodies to and fro, and the limitations of the human senses. The dramatist must not expect his audience to be able to see or hear two things at once, nor to be incapable of fatigue. And he must not expect his interpreters to stroll round or come on or go off in a satisfactory manner unless he provides them with satisfactory reasons for strolling round, coming on, or going off. Lastly, he must not expect his interpreters to achieve physical impossibilities. The dramatist who sends a pretty woman off in street attire

Arnold Bennett

and seeks to bring her on again in thirty seconds fully dressed for a court ball may fail in stage technique, but he has not proved that stage technique is tremendously difficult; he has proved something quite else.

The Author's Craft
III

One reason why a play is easier to write than a novel is that a play is shorter than a novel. On the average, one may say that it takes six plays to make the matter of a novel. Other things being equal, a short work of art presents fewer difficulties than a longer one. The contrary is held true by the majority, but then the majority, having never attempted to produce a long work of art, are unqualified to offer an opinion. It is said that the most difficult form of poetry is the sonnet. But the most difficult form of poetry is the epic. The proof that the sonnet is the most difficult form is alleged to be in the fewness of perfect sonnets. There are, however, far more perfect sonnets than perfect epics. A perfect sonnet may be a heavenly accident. But such accidents can never happen to writers of epics. Some years ago we had an enormous palaver about the "art of the short story," which numerous persons who had omitted to write novels pronounced to be more difficult than the novel. But the fact remains that there are scores of perfect short stories, whereas it is doubtful whether anybody but Turgenev ever did write a perfect novel. A short form is easier to manipulate than a long form, because its construction is less complicated, because the balance of its proportions can be more easily corrected by means of a rapid survey, because it is lawful and even necessary in it to leave undone many things which are very hard to do, and because the emotional strain is less prolonged. The most difficult thing in all art is to maintain the imaginative tension unslackened throughout a considerable period.

Then, not only does a play contain less matter than a novel—it is further simplified by the fact that it contains fewer kinds of matter, and less subtle kinds of matter. There are numerous delicate and difficult affairs of craft that the dramatist need not think about at all. If he attempts to go beyond a certain very mild degree of subtlety, he is merely wasting his time. What passes for subtle on the stage would have a very obvious air in a novel, as some dramatists have unhappily discovered. Thus whole continents of danger may be shunned by the dramatist, and instead of being scorned for his cowardice he will be very rightly applauded for his artistic discretion. Fortunate predicament! Again, he need not—indeed, he must not—save in a primitive and hinting manner, concern himself with "atmosphere." He may roughly suggest one, but if he begins on the feat of "creating" an atmosphere (as it is called), the last suburban train will have departed before he has reached the crisis of the play. The last suburban train is the best friend of the dramatist, though the fellow seldom has the sense to see it. Further, he is saved all de scriptive work. See a novelist harassing himself into his grave over the description of a landscape, a room, a gesture—while the dramatist grins. The dramatist may have to imagine a landscape, a room, or a gesture; but he has not got to write it—and it is the writing which hastens death. If a dramatist and a novelist set out to portray a clever woman, they are almost equally matched, because each has to make the creature say things and do things. But if they set out to portray a charming woman, the dramatist can recline in an easy chair and smoke while the novelist is ruining temper, digestion and eyesight, and spreading terror in his household by his moodiness and unapproachability. The electric light burns in the novelist's study at three a.m.,—the novelist is still endeavouring to convey by means of words the extraordinary fascination that his heroine could exercise over mankind by the mere act of walking into a room; and he never has really succeeded and never will. The dramatist writes curtly, "Enter Millicent." All are anxious to do the dramatist's job for him. Is the play being read at home—the reader eagerly and with brilliant success puts his imagination to work and completes a charming

The Author's Craft

Millicent after his own secret desires. (Whereas he would coldly decline to add one touch to Millicent were she the heroine of a novel.) Is the play being performed on the stage—an experienced, conscientious, and perhaps lovely actress will strive her hardest to prove that the dramatist was right about Millicent's astounding fascination. And if she fails, nobody will blame the dramatist; the dramatist will receive naught but sympathy.

And there is still another region of superlative difficulty which is narrowly circumscribed for the spoilt dramatist: I mean the whole business of persuading the public that the improbable is probable. Every work of art is and must be crammed with improbabilities and artifice; and the greater portion of the artifice is employed in just this trickery of persuasion. Only, the public of the dramatist needs far less persuading than the public of the novelist. The novelist announces that Millicent accepted the hand of the wrong man, and in spite of all the novelist's corroborative and exegetical detail the insulted reader declines to credit the statement and condemns the incident as unconvincing. The dramatist decides that Millicent must accept the hand of the wrong man, and there she is on the stage in flesh and blood, veritably doing it! Not easy for even the critical beholder to maintain that Millicent could not and did not do such a silly thing when he has actually with his eyes seen her in the very act! The dramatist, as usual, having done less, is more richly rewarded by results.

Of course it will be argued, as it has always been argued, by those who have not written novels, that it is precisely the "doing less"—the leaving out—that constitutes the unique and fearful difficulty of dramatic art. "The skill to leave out"—lo! the master faculty of the dramatist! But, in the first place, I do not believe that, having regard to the relative scope of the play and of the novel, the necessity for leaving out is more acute in the one than in the other. The adjective "photographic" is as absurd applied to the novel as to the play. And, in the second place, other factors being equal, it is less exhausting, and it requires less skill, to refrain from doing than to do. To know when to refrain from doing may be hard, but positively to do is even harder. Sometimes, listening to partisans of the drama, I have been moved to suggest that, if the art of omission is so wondrously difficult, a dramatist who practised the habit of omitting to write anything whatever ought to be hailed as the supreme craftsman.

The Author's Craft
IV

The more closely one examines the subject, the more clear and certain becomes the fact that there is only one fundamental artistic difference between the novel and the play, and that difference (to which I shall come later) is not the difference which would be generally named as distinguishing the play from the novel. The apparent differences are superficial, and are due chiefly to considerations of convenience.

Whether in a play or in a novel the creative artist has to tell a story—using the word story in a very wide sense. Just as a novel is divided into chapters, and for a similar reason, a play is divided into acts. But neither chapters nor acts are necessary. Some of Balzac's chief novels have no chapter-divisions, and it has been proved that a theatre audience can and will listen for two hours to "talk," and even recitative singing, on the stage, without a pause. Indeed, audiences, under the compulsion of an artist strong and imperious enough, could, I am sure, be trained to marvellous feats of prolonged receptivity. However, chapters and acts are usual, and they involve the same constructional processes on the part of the artist. The entire play or novel must tell a complete story—that is, arouse a curiosity and reasonably satisfy it, raise a main question and then settle it. And each act or other chief division must tell a definite portion of the story, satisfy part of the curiosity, settle part of the question. And each scene or other minor division must do the same according to its scale. Everything basic that applies to the technique of the novel applies equally to the technique of the play.

In particular, I would urge that a play, any more than a novel, need not be dramatic, employing the term as it is usually employed. In so far as it suspends the listener's interest, every tale, however told, may be said to be dramatic. In this sense *The Golden Bowl* is dramatic; so are *Dominique* and *Persuasion* . A play need not be more dramatic than that. Very emphatically a play need not be dramatic in the stage sense. It need never induce interest to the degree of excitement. It need have nothing that resembles what would be recognisable in the theatre as a situation. It may amble on—and it will still be a play, and it may succeed in pleasing either the fastidious hundreds or the unfastidious hundreds of thousands, according to the talent of the author. Without doubt mandarins will continue for about a century yet to excommunicate certain plays from the category of plays. But nobody will be any the worse. And dramatists will go on proving that whatever else divides a play from a book, "dramatic quality" does not. Some arch-Mandarin may launch at me one of those mandarinic epigram matic questions which are supposed to overthrow the adversary at one dart. "Do you seriously mean to argue, sir, that drama need not be dramatic?" I do, if the word dramatic is to be used in the mandarinic signification. I mean to state that some of the finest plays of the modern age differ from a psychological novel in nothing but the superficial form of telling. Example, Henri Becque's *La Parisienne* , than which there is no better. If I am asked to give my own definition of the adjective "dramatic," I would say that that story is dramatic which is told in dialogue imagined to be spoken by actors and actresses on the stage, and that any narrower definition is bound to exclude some genuine plays universally accepted as such—even by mandarins. For be it noted that the mandarin is never consistent.

My definition brings me to the sole technical difference between a play and a novel—in the play the story is told by means of a dialogue. It is a difference less important than it seems, and not invariably even a sure point of distinction between the two kinds of narrative. For a novel may consist exclusively of dialogue. And plays may contain other matter than dialogue. The classic chorus is not dialogue. But nowadays we should consider the device of the chorus to be clumsy, as, nowadays, it indeed would be. We have grown very ingenious and clever at the trickery of making characters talk to the audience and explain themselves and their past history while seemingly innocent of any such intention. And here, I admit, the dramatist has to face a difficulty special to himself, which the novelist can avoid. I believe it to be the sole difficulty which is peculiar to the drama, and that it is not acute is proved by the ease with which third-rate dramatists have generally vanquished it. Mandarins are wont to assert that the dramatist is also handicapped by the necessity for rigid economy in the use of material. This is not so. Rigid economy in the use of material is equally advisable in every form of art. If it is a necessity, it is a necessity which all artists flout from time to time, and occasionally with gorgeous results, and the successful dramatist has hitherto not been less guilty of flouting it than the novelist or any other artist.

Arnold Bennett
V

And now, having shown that some alleged differences between the play and the novel are illusory, and that a certain technical difference, though possibly real, is superficial and slight, I come to the fundamental difference between them—a difference which the laity does not suspect, which is seldom insisted upon and never sufficiently, but which nobody who is well versed in the making of both plays and novels can fail to feel profoundly. The emotional strain of writing a play is not merely less prolonged than that of writing a novel, it is less severe even while it lasts, lower in degree and of a less purely creative character. And herein is the chief of all the reasons why a play is easier to write than a novel. The drama does not belong exclusively to literature, because its effect depends on something more than the composition of words. The dramatist is the sole author of a play, but he is not the sole creator of it. Without him nothing can be done, but, on the other hand, he cannot do everything himself. He begins the work of creation, which is finished either by creative interpreters on the stage, or by the creative imagination of the reader in the study. It is as if he carried an immense weight to the landing at the turn of a flight of stairs, and that thence upward the lifting had to be done by other people. Consider the affair as a pyramidal structure, and the dramatist is the base—but he is not the apex. A play is a collaboration of creative faculties. The egotism of the dramatist resents this uncomfortable fact, but the fact exists. And further, the creative faculties are not only those of the author, the stage-director ("producer") and the actors—the audience itself is unconsciously part of the collaboration.

Hence a dramatist who attempts to do the whole work of creation before the acting begins is an inartistic usurper of the functions of others, and will fail of proper

The Author's Craft

accomplishment at the end. The dramatist must deliberately, in performing his share of the work, leave scope for a multitude of alien faculties whose operations he can neither precisely foresee nor completely control. The point is not that in the writing of a play there are various sorts of matters—as we have already seen—-which the dramatist must ignore; the point is that even in the region proper to him he must not push the creative act to its final limit. He must ever remember those who are to come after him. For instance, though he must visualise a scene as he writes it, he should not visualise it completely, as a novelist should. The novelist may perceive vividly the faces of his personages, but if the playwright insists on seeing faces, either he will see the faces of real actors and hamper himself by moulding the scene to suit such real actors, or he will perceive imaginary faces, and the ultimate interpretation will perforce falsify his work and nullify his intentions. This aspect of the subject might well be much amplified, but only for a public of practising dramatists.

VI

When the play is "finished," the processes of collaboration have yet to begin. The serious work of the dramatist is over, but the most desolating part of his toil awaits him. I do not refer to the business of arranging with a theatrical manager for the production of the play. For, though that generally partakes of the nature of tragedy, it also partakes of the nature of amusing burlesque, owing to the fact that theatrical managers are—no doubt inevitably—theatrical. Nevertheless, even the theatrical manager, while disclaiming the slightest interest in anything more vital to the stage than the box-office, is himself in some degree a collaborator, and is the first to show to the dramatist that a play is not a play till it is performed. The manager reads the play, and, to the dramatist's astonishment, reads quite a different play from that which the dramatist imagines he wrote. In particular the manager reads a play which can scarcely hope to succeed—indeed, a play against whose chances of success ten thousand powerful reasons can be adduced. It is remarkable that a manager nearly always foresees failure in a manuscript, and very seldom success. The manager's profoundest instinct—self-preservation again!—is to refuse a play; if he accepts, it is against the grain, against his judgment—and out of a mad spirit of adventure. Some of the most glittering successes have been rehearsed in an atmosphere of settled despair. The dramatist naturally feels an immense contempt for the opinions artistic and otherwise of the manager, and he is therein justified. The manager's vocation is not to write plays, nor (let us hope) to act in them, nor to direct the rehearsals of them, and even his knowledge of the vagaries of his own box-office has often proved to be pitiably delusive. The manager's true and only vocation is to refrain from producing plays. Despite all this, however, the manager has already collaborated in the play. The

The Author's Craft

dramatist sees it differently now. All sorts of new considerations have been presented to him. Not a word has been altered; but it is noticeably another play. Which is merely to say that the creative work on it which still remains to be done has been more accurately envisaged. This strange experience could not happen to a novel, because when a novel is written it is finished.

And when the director of rehearsals, or producer, has been chosen, and this priceless and mysterious person has his first serious confabulation with the author, then at once the play begins to assume new shapes—contours undreamt of by the author till that startling moment. And even if the author has the temerity to conduct his own rehearsals, similar disconcerting phenomena will occur; for the author as a producer is a different fellow from the author as author. The producer is up against realities. He, first, renders the play concrete, gradually condenses its filmy vapours into a solid element.... He suggests the casting. "What do you think of X. for the old man?" asks the producer. The author is staggered. Is it conceivable that so renowned a producer can have so misread and misunderstood the play? X. would be preposterous as the old man. But the producer goes on talking. And suddenly the author sees possibilities in X. But at the same time he sees a different play from what he wrote. And quite probably he sees a more glorious play. Quite probably he had not suspected how great a dramatist he is.... Before the first rehearsal is called, the play, still without a word altered, has gone through astounding creative transmutations; the author recognises in it some likeness to his beloved child, but it is the likeness of a first cousin.

At the first rehearsal, and for many rehearsals, to an extent perhaps increasing, perhaps decreasing, the dramatist is forced into an apologetic and self-conscious mood; and his mien is something between that of a criminal who has committed a horrid offence and that of a father over the crude body of a new-born child. Now in truth he deeply realises that the play is a collaboration. In extreme cases he may be brought to see that he himself is one of the less important factors in the collaboration. The first preoccupation of the interpreters is not with his play at all, but—quite rightly—with their own careers; if they were not honestly convinced that their own careers were the chief genuine excuse for the existence of the theatre and the play they would not act very well. But, more than that, they do not regard his play as a sufficient vehicle for the furtherance of their careers. At the most favourable, what they secretly think is that if they are permitted to exercise their talents on his play there is a chance that they may be able to turn it into a sufficient vehicle for the furtherance of their careers. The attitude of every actor towards his part is: "My part is not much of a part as it stands, but if my individuality is allowed to get into free contact with it, I may make something brilliant out of it." Which attitude is a proper attitude, and an attitude in my opinion justified by the facts of the case. The actor's phrase is that he *creates* a part, and he is right. He completes the labour of creation begun by the author and continued by the producer, and if reasonable liberty is not accorded to him—if either the author or the producer attempts to do too much of the creative work—the result cannot be satisfactory.

As the rehearsals proceed the play changes from day to day. However autocratic the producer, however obstinate the dramatist, the play will vary at each rehearsal like a large cloud in a gentle wind. It is never the same play for two days together. Nor is this surprising, seeing that every day and night a dozen, or it may be two dozen, human beings endowed with the creative gift are creatively working on it. Every dramatist who is candid with himself—I do not suggest that he should be candid to the theatrical world—well knows that though his play is often worsened by his collaborators it is also often improved,—and improved in the most mysterious and dazzling manner—without a word being altered. Producer and actors do not merely suggest possibilities, they execute them. And the author is confronted by artistic phenomena for which lawfully he may not claim credit. On the other hand, he may be confronted by inartistic phenomena in respect to which lawfully he is blameless, but which he cannot prevent; a rehearsal is like a battle,—certain persons are theoretically in control, but in fact the thing principally fights itself. And thus the creation goes on until the dress-rehearsal, when it seems to have come to a stop. And the dramatist lying awake in the night reflects, stoically, fatalistically: "Well, that is the play that they have made of *my* play!" And he may be pleased or he may be disgusted. But if he attends the first performance he cannot fail to notice, after the first few minutes of it, that he was quite mistaken, and that what the actors are performing is still another play. The audience is collaborating.

Arnold Bennett

The Author's Craft

Arnold Bennett

Part IV The Artist and the Public

I

I can divide all the imaginative writers I have ever met into two classes—those who admitted and sometimes proclaimed loudly that they desired popularity; and those who expressed a noble scorn or a gentle contempt for popularity. The latter, however, always failed to conceal their envy of popular authors, and this envy was a phenomenon whose truculent bitterness could not be surpassed even in political or religious life. And indeed, since (as I have held in a previous chapter) the object of the artist is to share his emotions with others, it would be strange if the normal artist spurned popularity in order to keep his emotions as much as possible to himself. An enormous amount of dishonest nonsense has been and will be written by uncreative critics, of course in the higher interests of crea tive authors, about popularity and the proper attitude of the artist thereto. But possibly the attitude of a first-class artist himself may prove a more valuable guide.

The *Letters of George Meredith* (of which the first volume is a magnificent unfolding of the character of a great man) are full of references to popularity, references overt and covert. Meredith could never—and quite naturally—get away from the idea of popularity. He was a student of the English public, and could occasionally be unjust to it. Writing to M. André Raffalovich (who had sent him a letter of appreciation) in November, 1881, he said: "I venture to judge by your name that you are at most but half English. I can consequently believe in the feeling you express for the work of an unpopular writer. Otherwise one would incline to be sceptical, for the English are given to practical jokes, and to stir up the vanity of authors who are supposed to languish in the shade amuses them." A remark curiously unfair to the small, faithful band of admirers which Meredith then had. The whole letter, while warmly and touchingly grateful, is gloomy. Further on in it he says: "Good work has a fair chance to be recognised in the end, and if not, what does it matter?" But there is constant proof that it did matter very much. In a letter to William Hardman, written when he was well and hopeful, he says: "Never mind: if we do but get the public ear, oh, my dear old boy!" To Captain Maxse, in reference to a vast sum of £8,000 paid by the *Cornhill* people to George Eliot (for an unreadable novel), he exclaims: "Bon Dieu! Will aught like this ever happen to me?"

And to his son he was very explicit about the extent to which unpopularity "mattered": "As I am unpopular I am ill-paid, and therefore bound to work double tides, hardly ever able to lay down the pen. This affects my weakened stomach, and so the round of the vicious circle is looped." (Vol. I., p. 322.) And in another letter to Arthur Meredith about the same time he sums up his career thus: "As for me, I have failed, and I find little to make the end undesirable." (Vol. I., p. 318.) This letter is dated June 23rd, 1881. Meredith was then fifty-three years of age. He had written *Modern Love*, *The Shaving of Shagpat*, *The Ordeal of Richard Feverel*, *Rhoda Fleming*, *The Egoist* and other masterpieces. He knew that he had done his best and that his best was very fine. It would be difficult to credit that he did not privately deem himself one of the masters of English literature and destined to what we call immortality. He had the enthusiastic appreciation of some of the finest minds of the epoch. And yet, "As for me, I have failed, and I find little to make the end undesirable."

Arnold Bennett

But he had not failed in his industry, nor in the quality of his work, nor in achieving self-respect and the respect of his friends. He had failed only in one thing—immediate popularity.

The Author's Craft
II

Assuming then that an author is justified in desiring immediate popularity, instead of being content with poverty and the unheard plaudits of posterity, another point presents itself. Ought he to limit himself to a mere desire for popularity, or ought he actually to do something, or to refrain from doing something, to the special end of obtaining popularity? Ought he to say: "I shall write exactly what and how I like, without any regard for the public; I shall consider nothing but my own individuality and powers; I shall be guided solely by my own personal conception of what the public ought to like"? Or ought he to say: "Let me examine this public, and let me see whether some compromise between us is not possible"?

Certain authors are never under the necessity of facing the alternative. Occasionally, by chance, a genius may be so fortunately constituted and so brilliantly endowed that he captures the public at once, prestige being established, and the question of compromise never arises. But this is exceedingly rare. On the other hand, many mediocre authors, exercising the most complete sincerity, find ample appreciation in the vast mediocrity of the public, and are never troubled by any problem worse than the vagaries of their fountain-pens. Such authors enjoy in plenty the gewgaw known as happiness. Of nearly all really original artists, however, it may be said that they are at loggerheads with the public—as an almost inevitable consequence of their originality; and for them the problem of compromise or no-compromise acutely exists.

George Meredith was such an artist. George Meredith before anything else was a poet. He would have been a better poet than a novelist, and I believe that he thought so. The public did not care for his poetry. If he had belonged to the no-compromise school, whose adherents usually have the effrontery to claim him, he would have said: "I shall keep on writing poetry, even if I have to become a stockbroker in order to do it." But when he was only thirty-three—a boy, as authors go—he had already tired of no-compromise. He wrote to Augustus Jessopp: "It may be that in a year or two I shall find time for a full sustained Song.... The worst is that having taken to prose delineations of character and life, one's affections are divided.... And in truth, being a servant of the public, *I must wait till my master commands before I take seriously to singing* ." (Vol. I., p. 45.) Here is as good an example as one is likely to find of a first-class artist openly admitting the futility of writing what will not be immediately read, when he can write something else, less to his taste, that will be read. The same sentiment has actuated an immense number of first-class creative artists, including Shakspere, who would have been a rare client for a literary agent.... So much for refraining from doing the precise sort of work one would prefer to do because it is not appreciated by the public.

There remains the doing of a sort of work against the grain because the public appreciates it—otherwise the pot-boiler. In 1861 Meredith wrote to Mrs Ross: "I am engaged in extra potboiling work which enables me to do this," i.e., to write an occasional long poem. (Vol. I., p. 52.) Oh, base compromise! Seventeen years later he wrote to R.L. Stevenson: "Of potboilers let none speak. Jove hangs them upon necks that could soar above his heights but for the accursed weight." (Vol. I., p. 291.) It may be said that Meredith was forced to write potboilers. He was no more forced to write potboilers than any other author. Sooner than wallow in that shame, he might have earned money in more difficult ways. Or he might have indulged in that starvation so heartily prescribed for authors by a plutocratic noble who occasionally deigns to employ the

English tongue in prose. Meredith subdued his muse, and Meredith wrote potboilers, because he was a first-class artist and a man of profound common sense. Being extremely creative, he had to arrive somehow, and he remembered that the earth is the earth, and the world the world, and men men, and he arrived as best he could. The great majority of his peers have acted similarly.

The truth is that an artist who demands appreciation from the public on his own terms, and on none but his own terms, is either a god or a conceited and impractical fool. And he is somewhat more likely to be the latter than the former. He wants too much. There are two sides to every bargain, including the artistic. The most fertile and the most powerful artists are the readiest to recognise this, because their sense of proportion, which is the sense of order, is well developed. The lack of the sense of proportion is the mark of the *petit maître* . The sagacious artist, while respecting himself, will respect the idiosyncrasies of his public. To do both simultaneously is quite possible. In particular, the sagacious artist will respect basic national prejudices. For example, no first-class English novelist or dramatist would dream of allowing to his pen the freedom in treating sexual phenomena which Continental writers enjoy as a matter of course. The British public is admittedly wrong on this important point—hypocritical, illogical and absurd. But what would you? You cannot defy it; you literally cannot. If you tried, you would not even get as far as print, to say nothing of library counters. You can only get round it by ingenuity and guile. You can only go a very little further than is quite safe. You can only do one man's modest share in the education of the public.

In Valery Larbaud's latest novel, *A.O. Barnabooth,* occurs a phrase of deep wisdom about women: " *La femme est une grande realite, comme la guerre* ." It might be applied to the public. The public is a great actuality,

Arnold Bennett

like war. If you are a creative and creating artist, you cannot ignore it, though it can ignore you. There it is! You can do something with it, but not much. And what you do not do with it, it must do with you, if there is to be the contact which is essential to the artistic function. This contact may be closened and completed by the artist's cleverness—the mere cleverness of adaptability which most first-class artists have exhibited. You can wear the fashions of the day. You can tickle the ingenuous beast's ear in order to distract his attention while you stab him in the chest. You can cajole money out of him by one kind of work in order to gain leisure in which to force him to accept later on something that he would prefer to refuse. You can use a thousand devices on the excellent simpleton.... And in the process you may degrade your self to a mere popularity-hunter! Of course you may; as you may become a drunkard through drinking a glass of beer. Only, if you have anything to say worth saying, you usually don't succumb to this danger. If you have anything to say worth saying, you usually manage somehow to get it said, and read. The artist of genuine vocation is apt to be a wily person. He knows how to sacrifice inessentials so that he may retain essentials. And he can mysteriously put himself even into a potboiler. *Clarissa Harlowe* , which influenced fiction throughout Europe, was the direct result of potboiling. If the artist has not the wit and the strength of mind to keep his own soul amid the collisions of life, he is the inferior of a plain, honest merchant in stamina, and ought to retire to the upper branches of the Civil Service.

The Author's Craft
III

When the author has finished the composition of a work, when he has put into the trappings of the time as much of his eternal self as they will safely hold, having regard to the best welfare of his creative career as a whole, when, in short, he has done all that he can to ensure the fullest public appreciation of the essential in him—there still remains to be accomplished something which is not unimportant in the entire affair of obtaining contact with the public. He has to see that the work is placed before the public as advantageously as possible. In other words, he has to dispose of the work as advantageously as possible. In other words, when he lays down the pen he ought to become a merchant, for the mere reason that he has an article to sell, and the more skilfully he sells it the better will be the result, not only for the public appreciation of his message, but for himself as a private individual and as an artist with further activities in front of him.

Now this absolutely logical attitude of a merchant towards one's finished work infuriates the dilettanti of the literary world, to whom the very word "royalties" is anathema. They apparently would prefer to treat literature as they imagine Byron treated it, although as a fact no poet in a short life ever contrived to make as many pounds sterling out of verse as Byron made. Or perhaps they would like to return to the golden days when the author had to be "patronised" in order to exist; or even to the mid-nineteenth century, when practically all authors save the most successful—and not a few of the successful also—failed to obtain the fair reward of their work. The dilettanti's snobbishness and sentimentality prevent them from admitting that, in a democratic age, when an author is genuinely appreciated, either he makes money or he is the foolish victim of a scoundrel. They are fond of saying that agreements and royalties have nothing to do with literature. But agreements and royalties have a very great deal to do with literature. Full contact between artist and public depends largely upon publisher or manager being compelled to be efficient and just. And upon the publisher's or manager's efficiency and justice depend also the dignity, the leisure, the easy flow of coin, the freedom, and the pride which are helpful to the full fruition of any artist. No artist was ever assisted in his career by the yoke, by servitude, by enforced monotony, by overwork, by economic inferiority. See Meredith's correspondence everywhere.

Nor can there be any satisfaction in doing badly that which might be done well. If an artist writes a fine poem, shows it to his dearest friend, and burns it—I can respect him. But if an artist writes a fine poem, and then by sloppiness and snobbishness allows it to be inefficiently published, and fails to secure his own interests in the transaction, on the plea that he is an artist and not a merchant, then I refuse to respect him. A man cannot fulfil, and has no right to fulfil, one function only in this complex world. Some, indeed many, of the greatest creative artists have managed to be very good merchants also, and have not been ashamed of the double *rôle* . To read the correspondence and memoirs of certain supreme artists one might be excused for thinking, indeed, that they were more interested in the *rôle* of merchant than in the other *rôle* ; and yet their work in no wise suffered. In the distribution of energy between the two *rôles* common sense is naturally needed. But the artist who has enough common sense—or, otherwise expressed, enough sense of reality—not to disdain the *rôle* of merchant will probably have enough not to exaggerate it. He may be reassured on one point—namely, that success in the *rôle* of merchant will never impair any self-satisfaction he may feel in the *rôle* of artist. The late discovery of a large public in America delighted Meredith and had a tonic effect on his whole system. It is often hinted, even if it is not often said, that great popularity ought to disturb the conscience of the artist. I do not believe it. If the conscience of the artist is not disturbed during the actual work itself, no subsequent phenomenon will or should disturb it. Once the artist is convinced of his artistic honesty, no public can be too large for his peace of mind. On the other hand, failure in the *rôle* of merchant will emphatically impair his self-satisfaction in the *rôle* of artist and his courage in the further pursuance of that *rôle* .

But many artists have admittedly no aptitude for merchantry. Not only is their sense of the bindingness of a bargain imperfect, but they are apt in business to behave in a puerile manner, to close an arrangement out of mere impatience, to be grossly undiplomatic, to be victimised by their vanity, to believe what they ought not to believe, to discredit what is patently true, to worry over negligible trifles, and generally to make a clumsy mess of their affairs. An artist may say: "I cannot work unless I have a free mind, and I cannot have a free mind if I am to be bothered all the time by details of business."

Apart from the fact that no artist who pretends also to be a man can in this world hope for a free mind, and that if he seeks it by neglecting his debtors he will be deprived of it by his creditors—apart from that, the artist's demand for a free mind is reasonable. Moreover, it is always a distressing sight to see a man trying to do what nature has not fitted him to do, and so doing it ill. Such artists, however—and they form possibly the majority—can always employ an expert to do their business for them, to cope on their behalf with the necessary middleman. Not that I deem the publisher or the theatrical manager to be by nature less upright than any other class of merchant. But the publisher and the theatrical manager have been subjected for centuries to a special and grave temptation. The ordinary merchant deals with other merchants—his equals in business skill. The publisher and the theatrical manager deal with what amounts to a race of children, of whom even arch-angels could not refrain from taking advantage.

When the democratisation of literature seriously set in, it inevitably grew plain that the publisher and the theatrical manager had very humanly been giving way to the temptation with which heaven in her infinite wisdom had pleased to afflict them,—and the Society of Authors came into being. A natural consequence of the general awakening was the self-invention of the literary agent. The Society of Authors, against immense obstacles, has performed wonders in the economic education of the creative artist, and therefore in the improvement of letters. The literary agent, against obstacles still more immense, has carried out the details of the revolution. The outcry—partly sentimental, partly snobbish, but mainly interested—was at first tremendous against these meddlers who would destroy the charming personal relations that used to exist between, for example, the author and the publisher. (The less said about those charming personal relations the better. Documents exist.) But the main battle is now over, and everyone concerned is beautifully aware who holds the field. Though much remains to be done, much has been done; and today the creative artist who, conscious of inability to transact his own affairs efficiently, does not obtain efficient advice and help therein, stands in his own light both as an artist and as a man, and is a reactionary force. He owes the practice of elementary common sense to himself, to his work, and to his profession at large.

The Author's Craft
IV

The same dilettante spirit which refuses to see the connection between art and money has also a tendency to repudiate the world of men at large, as being unfit for the habitation of artists. This is a still more serious error of attitude—especially in a storyteller. No artist is likely to be entirely admirable who is not a man before he is an artist. The notion that art is first and the rest of the universe nowhere is bound to lead to preciosity and futility in art. The artist who is too sensitive for contacts with the non-artistic world is thereby too sensitive for his vocation, and fit only to fall into gentle ecstasies over the work of artists less sensitive than himself.

The classic modern example of the tragedy of the artist who repudiates the world is Flaubert. At an early age Flaubert convinced himself that he had no use for the world of men. He demanded to be left in solitude and tranquillity. The morbid streak in his constitution grew rapidly under the fostering influences of peace and tranquillity. He was brilliantly peculiar as a schoolboy. As an old man of twenty-two, mourning over the vanished brio of youth, he carried morbidity to perfection. Only when he was travelling (as, for example, in Egypt) do his letters lose for a time their distemper. His love-letters are often ignobly inept, and nearly always spoilt by the crass provincialism of the refined and cultivated hermit. His mistress was a woman difficult to handle and indeed a Tartar in egotism, but as the recipient of Flaubert's love-letters she must win universal sympathy.

Full of a grievance against the whole modern planet, Flaubert turned passionately to ancient times (in which he would have been equally unhappy had he lived in them), and hoped to resurrect beauty when he had failed to see it round about him. Whether or not he did resurrect beauty is a point which the present age is now deciding. His fictions of modern life undoubtedly suffer from his detestation of the material; but considering his manner of existence it is marvellous that he should have been able to accomplish any of them, except *Un Coeur Simple* . The final one, *Bouvard et Pécuchet* , shows the lack of the sense of reality which must be the inevitable sequel of divorce from mankind. It is realism without conviction. No such characters as Bouvard and Pecuchet could ever have existed outside Flaubert's brain, and the reader's resultant impression is that the author has ruined a central idea which was well suited for a grand larkish extravaganza in the hands of a French Swift. But the spectacle of Flaubert writing in *mots justes* a grand larkish extravaganza cannot be conjured up by fancy.

    There are many sub-Flauberts rife in London. They are usually more critical than creative, but their influence upon creators, and especially the younger creators, is not negligible. Their aim in preciosity would seem to be to keep themselves unspotted from the world. They are for ever being surprised and hurt by the crudity and coarseness of human nature, and for ever bracing themselves to be not as others are. They would have incurred the anger of Dr. Johnson, and a just discipline for them would be that they should be cross-examined by the great bully in presence of a jury of butchers and sentenced accordingly. The morbid Flaubertian shrinking from reality is to be found to-day even in relatively robust minds. I was recently at a provincial cinema, and witnessed on the screen with a friend a wondrously ingenuous drama entitled "Gold is not All." My friend, who combines the callings of engineer and general adventurer with that of serving his country, leaned over to me in the darkness amid the violent applause, and said: "You know, this kind of thing always makes me ashamed of human nature." I answered him as Johnsonially as the circumstances would allow. Had he lived to the age of

The Author's Craft

fifty so blind that it needed a cinema audience to show him what the general level of human nature really is? Nobody has any right to be ashamed of human nature. Is one ashamed of one's mother? Is one ashamed of the cosmic process of evolution? Human nature *is* . And the more deeply the creative artist, by frank contacts, absorbs that supreme fact into his brain, the better for his work.

There is a numerous band of persons in London—and the novelist and dramatist are not infrequently drawn into their circle—who spend so much time and emotion in practising the rites of the religion of art that they become incapable of real existence. Each is a Stylites on a pillar. Their opinion on Leon Bakst, Francis Thompson, Augustus John, Cyril Scott, Maurice Ravel, Vuillard, James Stephens, E.A. Rickards, Richard Strauss, Eugen d'Albert, etc., may not be without value, and their genuine feverish morbid interest in art has its usefulness; but they know no more about reality than a Pekinese dog on a cushion. They never approach normal life. They scorn it. They have a horror of it. They class politics with the differential calculus. They have heard of Lloyd George, the rise in the price of commodities, and the eternal enigma, what is a sardine; but only because they must open a newspaper to look at the advertisements and announcements relating to the arts. The occasional frequenting of this circle may not be disadvantageous to the creative artist. But let him keep himself inoculated against its disease by constant steady plunges into the cold sea of the general national life. Let him mingle with the public, for God's sake! No phenomenon on this wretched planet, which after all is ours, is meet for the artist's shrinking scorn. And the average man, as to whom the artist's ignorance is often astounding, must for ever constitute the main part of the material in which he works.

Above all, let not the creative artist suppose that the antidote to the circle of dilettantism is the circle of social reform. It is not. I referred in the first chapter to the prevalent illusion that the republic has just now arrived at a crisis, and that if something is not immediately done disaster will soon be upon us. This is the illusion to which the circle of social reforms is naturally prone, and it is an illusion against which the common sense of the creative artist must mightily protest. The world is, without doubt, a very bad world; but it is also a very good world. The function of the artist is certainly concerned more with what is than with what ought to be. When all necessary reform has been accomplished our perfected planet will be stone-cold. Until then the artist's affair is to keep his balance amid warring points of view, and in the main to record and enjoy what is.... But is not the Minimum Wage Bill urgent? But when the minimum wage is as trite as the jury-system, the urgency of reform will still be tempting the artist too far out of his true path. And the artist who yields is lost.

Manufactured by Amazon.ca
Acheson, AB